SOCIAL JUSTICE REVISITED

By
Kamal Majumdar
M.Sc (Calcutta) M.Sc (London)

"Sarvajana Hitaya, Sarvajana Sukhaya"

*"Prosperity and Happiness
for Everyone"*

**Dedicated to
my parents, teachers and to
the mankind**

Disclaimer

This book is written for informational and educational purposes only. The writer does not hold any responsibility for interpretation or actions by anyone reading this book. The writer does not intend to spread hatred or class difference in the society. The author's only intention is to spread the message of love and social justice among its readers.

Published by new Generation Publishing in 2023, Copyright © Kamal Majumdar 2023

First Edition

ISBN
     Paperback 978-1-80369-910-3

www.newgeneration-publishing.com
New Generation Publishing

PREFACE

Writing this book came in my mind towards end of the pandemic. My sister Tanushree Majumdar gave me a lot of encouragement and support to write and publish this book. I thank her sincerely for all her inspiration. I also thank Mr. Sumeswar Das for his valueable inputs in this book. Social justice is a passion for me and will always be a passion as I myself, come from an underprivileged family. I also thank the printers and publishers sincerely for the good work they have done in publication of this book in a short notice. I hope the contents will be informative to readers and provoke thoughts. My efforts will be successful if the reader is encouraged to bring social justice in practice by helping the destitute, marginalized and the downtrodden.

Kamal Majumdar 15.05.2023

CONTENTS

CHAPTER-1 INTRODUCTION

Who am I? Where do I come from? Where will I go or end up? Do we really know? Or, we are constantly striving to seek an answer for a just and unselfish society. Are we progressing in the right direction? Or, we are increasingly involved in a rat race to find wealth and bury our happiness and others'. These are the questions that constantly pokes my mind in order to fulfill a dream come true. My thoughts, my passion goes in the direction what is often called — "an utopia." The wisdom of ancient sages in India told us to see the whole world in oneness. That is "the whole world is one big family". whatever affects us in one part of the world is definitely has a knock on effect on other parts of the world. See, how are we falling like dominos in 21st century to face the climate change. We have only materialistically progressed so far. Talking about the 5th industrial revolution, while many of our brethren living in the same society does not have access to basic amenities like food, clothing, medicine and shelter. It grieves my heart to think that for millions and millions of people across the globe the benefits of the first industrial revolution even today remains untouched.

What we need to do then? We need to create, work, organise, share and mobilise our resources.

We, further need to spread the eternal message of love and take care of each other. Also, we need to raise our moral standards and above all keep our integrity. Today, our modern society is very much dependant on advancement of technology. Technology makes us our live easier but I must say that technology for mankind should be in the hands of kindman. Otherwise, catastrophe happens.

Imperfect and biased system towards capitalism in many countries causing unsustainable developments. The systems are biased throughout the countries, throughout the world. It dictates to fight, encourages immorality and to deceit each other in the name of religion and politics. So, how could peace be sustainable? This is the big question in this century. Peace is not sustainable when countries cut their budget on welfare, education, healthcare and invest more and more money in defence, engineering and production. This trend is global and I, personally perceive this as a threat to sustainable global peace.

I am oppressed.

I am oppressed and I seek justice for every oppressed person around the planet. I feel social justice have not been done for me or my family. Do you feel the same? Then you are my co-passenger in this journey.

"To strive, to seek, to find and not to yield."

—Lord Tennyson.

This is the only mantra I am carrying in my heart since my childhood. I have seen life. My only advice to my brothers and sisters who feel the same that keep patience and do not give up. Patience is a virtue.

CHAPTER-2 ANCIENT WISDOM

Ancient philosophers like Aristotle Plato, Chanakya and many others across the globe inspired the humanity with great ideas. In range of vision, in reach of sympathy, they have thrown light to the mankind. It is very important to be able to think independently. However, the time tested wisdom and truth delivered by our forefathers should be passed down from generation to generation with humility and great respect. I remember chanting a prayer from my early school days that—

"Let us walk together, speak together and let our minds fill with togetherness."

The power of one is the power of unity. Let us feel the power of this prayer. Let there be heterogeneity in population, thoughts and culture. Unity in diversity will prevail and bring many good values in our society than considering our societies based solely on homogenity.

Also, it is very important to think holistically or in totality. Like, if we consider humanity and other creatures with sensitivity, we will nurture the nature and never our actions will hurt mother earth. All our efforts should be directed towards sustainable development even for the marginalized and the poor.

There are millions of people who lose their way in our society due to socio-economic adversity. We need to stop that. Swami Vivekananda once said, "If you give them half a loaf, they can change the whole world." His reach of sensitivity and feelings for poor and downtrodden was unparallel in the whole human history. His message was — "Serve God in Man".

This is not with a mindset of doing charity. This should be done with passion and love.

Let renunciation and service be our pillars of ideals. Then and then only, we can see a sea-change in our society in our life-time.

Let us not stop here. In Swami Vivekananda's own words

"Arise, awake and stop not till the goal is reached."

From Vedas to Vivekananda and Chanakya to Shri Chaitanya our heritage is wonderfully rich. The message is "LOVE". There is an ancient saying that I remember is

> **"Bahurupe sammukhe tomar chari kotha khujicho Ishwar ;**
> **Jibe prem kore jai jon, sei jon sebiche Ishwar."**

It means, "God is in front of us in may shapes and forms. Oh! dear seeker. The one who loves the jiba or living things is serving the God."

In other words "He prayeth best, who loveth best." —Samuel Taylor Coleridge

Shri Chaitanya told notorious brothers Jagai and Madhai, who had broken an earthen pot on his head and made him bleed "merechis kolshir kana, tai bole ki prem debone".

"Meaning : Although you have hurt me with an earthen pot, still I will give you love." Without Chaitanyadev, India or Bharat would have been disfigured and lost her identity. He appeared when Indian society was in a decaying and degenerating condition and prevented the society from rotting further down by spreading the message of love from Lord Shri Krishna for all living beings.

Plato :

"Justice is a condition of soul." Plato's philosophy was justice is a part of good life. This is true for the good life of the individual as well as the good life of the city. Plato appeared 2400 years ago. In his book Eudaimonia (which means "good spirit, happiness or welfare") stressed on four points :

1)   Think more (know yourself)
2)   Let your lover change you (True love is admiration)
3)   Decode the message of beauty (Beautiful objects educate our souls).
4)   Reform society.

In his book "The Republic" Plato said "Guardians" should be simple, modest and decent people. Here, he means guardian of the state. Goal :- Politicians should ultimately become philosphers and the king (ruler) should be like a philosopher.

Aristotle : Aristotle appeared in 384 B.C. He was the teacher of Alexander the great. Plato and Aristotle both agreed that justice is a part of good life, which is essentially true for the individual and the state or city. Moreover, in Aristotle's opinion, "Justice is treating equals equally and unequals unequally," i.e. giving additional support to the disadvantaged. Aristotle asked a few questions a) What makes people happy? b) What is art for? c) What are friends for? and d) how can ideas cut through in a busy world? He answered, a) moral goodness, virtues, b) catharsis (cleaning up of emotions, fear or pitty, showing more compassion) c) Friends could be seeking fun, strategic aquaintences or true friends who share virtues and cancel out each others defects. d) Aristotle pointed out that to cut through ideas in a busy world one has to be persuasive. Make your presentation funny and see the emotional side of it.

CHAPTER-3 SOCIO-ECONOMIC JUSTICE

Theories of socio-economic justice :

Time and again many great thinkers, moved by the socio-economic condition of people around them propounded many great ideas of social and economic justice — often called "utopia". Great phillosophers think profoundly to find remedies for social and economic evils. Mahatma Gandhi, Chanakya, Aristotle Plato to name a few. There are many socio-economic theories that have evolved around many centuries and has seen rise of many great empires. Capitalism, communism, socialism, utiliterianism, integral humanism and so on. Next, I am going to discuss why some of them have failed while some others sustained at least in part in this unequal world.

Man is inherently selfish. Integrity, discipline and unselfish upbringing from childhood makes men with character. Many men working towards a common goal for the good of fellow citizens makes a nation great. In order to build men of character dedication, renunciation and discipline are paramount. Otherwise, all-isms will fail. This is due to the reason that we have sufficient resources on earth to fulfil everybodies needs, but we do not have sufficient resource to fulfil even one person's greed.

Theories of social justice :

Communism :- Is an ideology which states the society should be classless, moneyless and stateless. Money should not be the driving force of peoples lives. Karl Marx during his time experienced the poor conditions of thousands of factory workers and in general poor people of the society who were used and manipulated to create wealth for the few rich factory owners. Karl Marx and Friedrich Engles published "The Communist Manifesto" in 1848 and said that capitalism would inevitably self destruct, to be replaced by socialism and ultimately communism.

Capitalism :- It is essentially an economic and political system in which a country's trade and economic system are owned and controlled by private entrepreneurs with the state having minimal control or regulation over it. Capitalism can cause inequality among people dividing the citizens in a class of 'haves' and 'have nots'. It can also cause damage to environment, boom & bust of the economy and excessive materialism.

Socialism :- Socialism is an idea in which the means of production and resources are owned by the public leading to a more just and equal society. Economic planning, objective to a classless society, state responsibility for basic necessities for everyone, equal opportunity, non existence of competition and pricing mechanism are the salient features of an ideal socialist state.

Libertarianism :- Libertarianism literally means to defend and protect freedom. Libertarian economy advices state not to dictate with the taxes or money from the citizens. It is more about promoting individual freedom. It does not advocates welfare or social security. It assumes, economic growth is directly related to personal happiness. However, there is no country that has came forward to accept and implement libertarianism.

Utilitarianism :- Jeremy Bentham propounded this theory. "The needs of the few could be sacrificed for the needs (happiness) of the many." His ideas were revolutionary in many ways at his time, but some serious flaws were observed. John Stuart Mill, his student tried to quantify this theory and said, "It is better to be a human being dissatisfied than a pig satisfied. In my opinion, 'one for all and all for one' is a better idea to correct utilitariainsm.

Integral Humanism :- Pandit Deendayal Upadhyay, an Indian economist, philosopher, sociologist and politician visioned this idea. It states that the human being remains at the centre of development. The aim of integral humanism is to ensure a dignified life for every human being while balancing the needs of the individual and the society.

There are two main philosophies in this theory, i.e. 'Chiti' and 'Virat'. One is the soul of Nation and another is growth and progress of the nation, He also propounded 'antodaya i.e. the development of the last person standing in the end of the queue.

Egalitarianism :- Egalitarianism states that give everyone a chance and make society fairer. But, the question is how? There are two pillars of egalitarianism which says, (1) Justice as equality and (2) Distributive justice. It states that equality of rights cannot be sacrificed in the name of increasing social / economic goods. Fair and equal opportunities requires equal educational opportunities. Prevention of extreme wealth and prevention of discrimination.

Anarchy :- Anarchy is not people running around the streets breaking store windows, but it is a conception of a very organised society with as little control and domination as possible. This was the view of Noam Chomsky. Mahatma Gandhi introduced a form of non-violent anarchy for the people of India against the British Raj to gain momentum in India's freedom movement like "non-co-operation" and "Quit India movement". Some people do use violence against the government as a tool and call it anarchy. In my opinion anarchy is good for freedom and egalitarianism but is difficult to perfect and put to practice.

CHAPTER-4 TAKING A DIRECTION

The great hindu monk Swami Vivekananda used to say "I am a socialist." His vision and sympathy for the poor and oppressed, marginalized and have nots was unparalled in human history. I, myself, a deeply spiritual human being believe in Swami Vivekananda's Socialism. He told his disciples "Serve God in Man". Mahatma Gandhi was focused on "Satyagraha", i.e. keenness to search and stick to the 'Truth'. Next, Pandit Deendayal Upadhayay propounded a new concept called "Integral humanism" which talk about self-development (chiti) and National development (Virat). 'Antodaya' is a term coined for the rise of the very marginalized of the society. Moreover, there is a spiritual element belonging to this idea. East will show light.

We do not want to create a Godless, excessive materialistic society. Nor we want to create a religiously bigot, male dominated, unequal, unhappy and unjust society. Our goal is to persevere, protect and promote the goodness of both eastern and western philosophies to progress, thrive, undo class differences and bring justice to the society as a whole.

Different models of social justice : Social justice can be broadly defined as learning to give. Giving in terms of distribution of wealth, opportunities and priviledge generally in a society to them who needs most. In other words, it also means 'levelling up' for the poor and disadvantaged. So far, many theories and models have been propounded by many thinkers, philosophers. From Aristotle to Karl Marx, from Chanakya to Swami Vivekananda. From great rulers like Ashoka to social reformers like Raja Ram Mohan Roy. We are in a much better world now than even a few hundred years before. However, much work still needs to be done in respect to social justice. Looking ahead,I am going to discuss a few successful models of social justice. Their success and challenges and try to find an universally acceptable path.

The Bhutan Model : Bhutan is a small Himalayan kingdom located between India, Bangladesh and Tibet. It is mainly dominated by Buddhist culture and has a constitutional monarchy. The kingdom is promoting democracy and is one of the three nations which are carbon negative on earth. The most important feature of Bhutan is that Bhutan is the happiest country on earth.

Salient features of Bhutan's development :-

A)   **Environmental conservation :** According to the Bhutanese constitution 65% of land must be covered by forest at all times. At present, it is over 70% of Bhutan's land mass. Hence, Bhutan is carbon negative.

B)   **Cultural promotion :-** Bhutanese society is quite conservative in nature. Mostly it is a Buddhist society and Bhutanese people wants to conserve their identity in Buddhism.

C)   **Sustainable and equitable development :**
Tobacco and plastic bags are banned in Bhutan. Food production is 100% organic. Focus is on sustainable development.

D)   **Good governance:**
Good governance is marked by universal education and healthcare. No homelessness, reducing inequality and promoting gross national happiness (GNH).

The Nordic Model :-
Iceland, Finland, Norway, Denmark and Sweden are Nordic countries. Comprehensive welfare system is supported by mutual trust and dialogue between government, employer and employee. The tax is usually high but the public welfare is also very good. Hence, the happiness index is also very high in these countries.

Salient features of Nordic model :- Tripartite collaboration. The main pillars of tripartite collaboration are :

A)   **Economic governance :-** Ruled by controlled spending, free trade, taxes are paid and employment opportunities are increasingly available. Countries focusing on their strength or comparative advantage.

B)   **Public welfare :-** More people in the workforce means more taxes are collected for a comprehensive welfare system.

C)   **Organised working :-** Strong and responsible organisations, at all domains push up wages at a measured and responsible rate.

Challenges and future opportunities :- Vulnerability of welfare system due to increasingly aging population.

- Inequalities increasing
- Falling trade union
- Expanded labour market marked by illicit work and social dumping.

Way forward :- Way forward is globalization leading to lawful immigration and population development. Technology development and addressing issues of climate change.

CHAPTER-5 ROAD TO PROSPERITY : WEALTH REDISTRIBUTION AND SOCIAL JUSTICE

Wealth inequality has spiralled out of control in the recent years. The wealth gap has ever so increased in the whole world. Concentration of wealth is dangerous for democracy and meritocracy. Also it is dangerous for racial and gender equality. It furthur leads to crony capitalism. The answer is to tax wealth. This was introduced by President Roosvelt in the United States. Also capital gains tax needs to be introduced across the spectrum. Now, how to reduce the gap? Let us use the wisdom of President Roosevelt. We need a new wealth tax. Also, to close the loopholes of tax avoidance in the tax system. The pandemic has radically changed the world and forced us to rethink.

World economic forum agenda 2022 :-

1)   Pandemic recovery.

2)   Tackling climate change.

3)   Building a better future for work.

4)   Accelerating stakeholder capitalism.

5)   Harnessing the technologies of the Fourth Industrial Revolution.

The bottom line is to protect the most vulnerable first. However, do not expect phillanthropy from every rich like Bill Gates. The pressing need is to protect the bottom half of the 8 billion population that inhabits the earth today.

Impact of war and terrorism :- War is pathetic. There is no point of glorifying a war. Also, terrorism in any form needs to be tackled and confronted in its source. It is very important to cling on to the ideologies that counters terrorism and war. The innocent and vulnerable are most affected by these predator ideologies. Mahatma Gandhi once told that "if you ask an eye for an eye, the world would be blind in no time." So, we have to nurture the ideals of peace and forgiveness. Otherwise, whatever progress we may make will be lost forever.

Also, it is disastrous for climate change, sustainability and social justice for the 8 billion inhabitants of this beautiful planet earth.

Tackling crime and corruption :- Tackling crime and corruption is not the last thing in my mind. It has a high priority of all our tangible and untangible needs. We need better local and international policing with the aid of technology to keep one step ahead of lone wolves and organised crimes. Drugs, crime and corruption has caused a predicament situation in the developed and developing countries alike. No one is secure in this world if we do not press our acceleration to tackle crime and corruption immediately. Last but not the least, crime and corruption eats away all the sustainable development we may try to achieve for the rich and poor alike. This will bring sustainable social justice for once and for all.

CHAPTER-6 CONCLUSION

In conclusion, it may be said that whatever we do to turn this society to an utopian society turns out to be a dystopia if human greed and corruption are not controlled. This is why I sat down to write this book with the only aim to enlight people's minds in the right direction. No amount of talk or discussion will be effective if we do not prepare ourselves philanthropically. This book attempts to lighten one lamp to another lamp, i.e. putting philanthropy transferred from one mind to another mind. This is my aim and my effort will succeed if the readers can enlighten others minds with philosophy and philanthropy of social justice.

The beginning